LET
THE CHILDREN
COME

LET THE CHILDREN COME

Holy Communion

Reverend Dianne Langlois Dorsey

authorHOUSE®

AuthorHouse™ LLC
1663 Liberty Drive
Bloomington, IN 47403
www.authorhouse.com
Phone: 1-800-839-8640

Published by AuthorHouse 07/08/2014

ISBN: 978-1-4969-0353-2 (sc)
ISBN: 978-1-4969-0352-5 (e)

*Scripture quotations marked KJV are from the Holy Bible, King James
Version (Authorized Version). First published in 1611. Quoted from the KJV
Classic Reference Bible, Copyright © 1983 by The Zondervan Corporation.*

DEDICATION

I believe the Holy Spirit has been guiding me for the past several months, on how to focus and observe our children as they take Holy Communion. The purpose of this book is to help our little ones understand Holy Communion. Jesus called the Children to him and said, "Let the little ones come to me, and do not hinder them, for the kingdom of God belongs to such as these. I tell you the truth, anyone who will not receive the Kingdom of God like a little child will never enter it".

How do I begin writing this book? I'm not an authority on the Bible, but as a woman of God, filled with the Holy Spirit, I do feel I must help the children. "Communion", what is that?

As a child I too wanted to eat the cracker and drink the grape juice. But what did it mean? What did this ritual symbolize? Children, or should I say some children have a lot of play in them. Do they really pause while kneeling, to say thank you God for this day, for mama and daddy, food on our table, a home, breath and most of all thank you for Jesus. Some children may have nothing to eat, others may cry themselves to sleep at night. Maybe a cracker or wafer and some good old grape juice is just what they need. I think it's not just for the church alone to teach on why we take Holy Communion but also the parents. Holy Communion is serious, sacred and sanctified. Train up a child in the way he should go, and when he is old, he will not depart from it. He will remain on the right path.

Teach him about Holy Communion, and when it's time to partake in it he will understand why taking communion is important. A time to thank God for his goodness, grace and mercy through Jesus' broken body and the blood he has shed for us. The choice will be his, as he is taught to make the right decision. He will know why his decision to eat and drink of this table is important. It won't be because he sees others do it, but it will be to honor Jesus.

Invitation to Christian Discipleship, Prayer of Adoration, The Prayer Humiliation and The Consecration is read to everyone. As I stand in the pulpit, watching the children line up for Holy Communion, my pastor raises her hand in a gesture to "Let the children come." As they approach the altar with anticipation and smiles on their faces, they kneel and bow their heads in prayer. I often wonder if they really know why they are taking Holy Communion. Do they know what the wafer and juice represent? When I serve communion to the sick and shut in, I'm surrounded by children in the home, but do they understand? You see children copy what adults do. It is our duty to train our children in such matters as this.

Let me begin! God! Who is God? The dictionary describes God as being the supreme reality, creator and ruler of the universe, supreme, supernatural, powerful, and require worship. God is gracious and righteous and full of mercy (compassion, feeling pity). (Psalm 116:5) God is my strength, my defence, and the God of my mercy (loving). (Psalm 59:17) God is our salvation, our help, He is holy, mighty and awesome. God is eternal, change not, almighty, all knowing, present everywhere. God's home is in heaven (Isaiah 66:1).

God who made heaven and earth, created Adam and Eve in which sin was introduce to the world. Because of the sin of Adam, Eve and their son Cain who murdered his brother Abel, we are born with a sinful nature. This sinful nature causes us to commit sin. Behold, I was shaped (form) in iniquity (wickedness); and in sin did my mother conceive me (Psalm 51:5)

Now, my darlings let's talk about Jesus. God loves us so much, that he gave his only begotten Son, that whosoever believeth in him should not perish but have everlasting (eternal) life. For God did not send his son into the world to condemn but whoever does not believe stands condemned already, because he has not believed in the name of God's one and only Son. (John 3:16-18) God wanted to forgive us our sins, so he sent Jesus Christ to die on the cross so that we may live in heaven. Jesus preached "repentance" (to turn from sin) for the kingdom of heaven is near. (Matthew 4:17) When we do the will of God, we will enter the kingdom of heaven. (Matthew 4:21) Jesus offers us the keys of the kingdom. (Matthew 16:19) We will inherit the kingdom prepared for you from the foundation (creation) of the world. (Matthew 25:34) Jesus was sent to preach the good news of the kingdom of God. (Luke 4:43) Jesus wants us to eat and drink at his table in his kingdom. (Luke 22:30) I tell you the truth no one can enter the kingdom of God unless he is born of water and the Spirit.

Jesus shed His blood for our sins. He sacrificed his life for us. He took our sins, He knew no sin,

His Blood allows God's divine grace upon us. That if thou shalt confess with thy mouth the Lord Jesus, and shalt believe in your heart that God hath risen Him from the dead, thou shalt be saved. For with the heart man believeth unto righteousness; and with the mouth confession is made unto salvation. (Roman 10:9-10) When we get baptized, the body of sin is destroyed, and we walk in the newness of life. (Roman 6:4) Jesus wants us to follow Him, come by faith, come to be healed, come for hope and joy. Jesus was wounded for our transgressions (to go beyond the limits set by divine law). He was bruised for our iniquities (wickedness), the chastisement (to punish) of our peace was upon Him; and with His stripes (cutting) we are healed. (Isaiah 53:5) Jesus shed his blood for the remission of sins. (Matthew 26:28) Jesus Christ shed his blood as a sacrifice (a lamb to the slaughter), He took our sins upon Himself.

The physical agony was horrible, but even worse was the period of spiritual separation from God. Because of Jesus we will never have to experience eternal separation from God. We are Christ's very own chosen by God, so we should live lives worthy of the calling we have received from Christ. We should be gentle, patient, understanding, humble and peaceful. There is only one body and one Spirit, one hope, one Lord, one faith, one baptism, one God and Father of all. To each one of us grace has been given as Christ apportioned it. (Ephesians 4:4-7)

Christ gave some to be apostles, some to be prophets, some to be evangelists, and some to be pastors and teachers, to prepare God's people for works of service so that the body of Christ may be built up until we all reach unity in the faith and the knowledge of the Son of God and become mature, attaining to the whole measure of the fullness of Christ. (Ephesians 4:11-13)

NOW!!! Let the little children come to me, and do not hinder them for the kingdom of heaven belongs to such as these. (Matthew 19:14) Jesus wants little children to come because he loves them and because they have the kind of attitude needed to approach God. The receptiveness of little children is great, no stubbornness stand in the way of simple faith needed to believe in Jesus.

Submit humbly to Christ, have faith in Christ, be obedient, humble, and gentle.

Ask the children: (what the children told me about Holy Communion)

When I ask some of the children I came in contact with do they know why do they take Holy Communion?

Comments from the children: Do you know why we take communion?

Because others take it.

My mother told me to take it.

I like the wafer and juice.

I take it so I can go to heaven like jeepers creepers.

I don't know why I take it.

I was looking forward to drinking that grape juice.

Oh! This must be the day we drink the grape juice.

All I know is one Sunday we do this.

Some when ask, would shake their heads and hunch their shoulders as if to say no.

.

The Passover

The historic roots of the Passover are found in (Exodus 12:3-23). When the destroying angel swept through Egypt, he "passed over" the homes of the Israelites, which were identified by the blood of a lamb sprinkled on the doorposts. To the Christian, the Passover speaks of Jesus. Christ is our Passover Lamb who has been sacrificed for us. (1 Corinthians 5:7) Our redemption (to recover, free rescue) is linked to his shedding (flow from a cut or wound) Blood, Our Lamb of God. (John 1:29)

THE LORD'S SUPPER

The Lord's Supper represents the death of Christ for our sins. We are reminded of Christ's death and of his return. Our Faith is strengthened when we eat, drink and fellowship with other believers.

The early church remembered that Jesus instituted the Lord's Supper on the night of the Passover meal. (Luke 22:13) Just as Passover celebrated deliverance from slavery in Egypt, so the Lord's supper celebrates deliverance from sin by Christ' death. Bread and wine symbolize Christ's body and blood.

Paul gives specific instructions on how the Lord's Supper should be observed.

1. Thoughtfully (we proclaim Christ died for our sins)

2. Worthily, reverence and respect.

3. Examine ourselves for any unconfessed sin or resentful attitude.

4. Love for Christ

5. Be considerate of others.

6. Waiting until everyone is there and then eating in an orderly and unified manner (1 Corinthians 11:26,27,28,33)

The Lord's Supper, because it commemorates the Passover meal Jesus ate with his disciples, is the Eucharist (thanksgiving). In it we thank God for Christ's work for us.

Communion

We commune with God and with other believers. As we eat the bread and drink the wine, we should be quietly reflective as we recall Jesus death and his promise to come again. We should be grateful for God's wonderful gift to us, and joyful as we meet with Christ and the body of believers.

People under the old covenant (those who lived before Jesus) could approach God only through a priest and an animal sacrifice. Now, all people can come directly to God through faith because Jesus' death has made us acceptable in God's eyes. (Roman 3:21) Jesus is the final and ultimate sacrifice for sin. Rather than an unblemished lamb slain on the altar, the perfect Lamb of God was slain on the cross, a sinless sacrifice so that our sins could be forgiven once and for all. All those who believe in Christ become a new creature (human being) old things are passed away. All things become new. (2 Corinthians 5:17)

THE COVENANT OFFERS:

Healing, repentance, laying on of hands, resurrection and eternal judgment, gifts of the spirit, the Lord's Supper, marriage union, (they are no more twain (two), but one flesh, what therefore God hath joined together, let not man put <u>asunder</u> (into separate pieces), prayer and worship (Matthew 19)

My little ones, you must have a personal relationship with God. Search your hearts, ask forgiveness of sin, pray and study your Bible. Examine yourselves. Many people do not take communion because they feel guilty of sin, but we all have sinned. That's why Jesus died, so that we can be forgiven of our sins. If you have anything against anyone, forgive them. That is why at the altar, we bow our heads and ask forgiveness from the Lord. (1 Corinthians 11:27-30)

Jesus took bread, gave thanks (blessed it, broke it, and gave it to his disciples), saying: Take, and eat; This is my body. The he took the cup, gave thanks and offered it to them, saying "Drink from it, all of you. This is my blood of the covenant, which is poured out for many for the forgiveness of sins." (Matthew 26:26,

Luke 24:30-31) Remember as Christians we need a right relationship with the Lord and our brothers and sisters to take part in communion. Examine ourselves. (1 Corinthians 11:29-30)

Notes

Notes

Notes

Notes

Notes

Notes

Notes

Notes

Notes

Notes

Notes

Notes

Notes

Notes

Notes

Notes

Notes

Notes

Notes

ABOUT THE AUTHOR

Reverend Dianne Langlois Dorsey was born in New Orleans, LA.

She is the daughter of Leroy and Alberta Langlois. She is married to Irvin (YAYA), whom she describe as handsome and her soul mate. She has one daughter, Philana, a beautiful granddaughter, Greiana, and a handsome grandson Sherrod.

Dianne is the author of several books;: "Katrina" after the Storm," Sweet Inspiration Dove of Life, Angel on My Shoulder, Direction Which Way Is Up, Practical Living for the child,

Life after Adultery, and Let the Children come "Communion". The author of several songs: He'll Dry Your Eyes, "You Should Have Been There", "Holy Time." Dianne is a nurse, song writer, author, and a gospel singer. She has sung around New Orleans. Her goal is to record again and to continue writing books. Dianne lost everything in "Katrina", and is striving to rebuild her life after eight years. She believes that God has given everyone a job to do. As a child, I felt different, but mama always told me that I had favor with God and that he was always with me. I use to wonder if I were on the right planet. Hi! Silly how children think. I didn't really know what was going on in my life, believe me, I've been tested. Yes! I've been through the storm, and life's many more storms.

But God will see me through. You have to love everyone unconditionally. Since Katrina" Dianne has answered her calling into the ministry, she is now Reverend Dianne I ran until I couldn't run anymore, and I finally surrendered to God's calling on my life. And you know what, it's a good feeling to work for God and the benefits are great. When I retire, God promised me a place in his kingdom. To help you find your calling in life, just picture success, speak it and think positive. Go ahead and ask God to show you what to do. Step out on Faith, remember nothing is impossible for God. Only what you do for Christ will last.

Printed in the United States
By Bookmasters